After You

After You

BY DAVE CARLEY

After You
first published 1995 by
Scirocco Drama
An imprint of J. Gordon Shillingford Publishing Inc.
© 1993 Dave Carley

Cover design by Terry Gallagher/Doowah Design
Author photo by Michael Lee

Printed and bound in Canada by Hignell Printing Ltd.

Published with the assistance of The Canada Council.

Canadian Cataloguing in Publication Data

Carley, Dave, 1955-
After you

A play.
ISBN 1-896239-00-5

I. Title.
PS8555.A7397A47 1995 C842'.54   C95-910849-1
PR9199.3.C37A47 1995

For Margaret Carley and Alicia Perry, with love.

Characters

YOUNG ADELE: 20
YOUNG JEAN: 20
ADELE: late 70s
JEAN: late 70s
PAUL/JEFFERY: early 20s

Time

The summer months of 1938
Early September, mid-1990s

Setting

The Findlay islands on Lake Kawartha. It is strongly suggested that the set be non-representational.

Staging

The action of the play should be continuous and uninterrupted by blackouts and freezes. All of the characters can be aware of the other characters, at any or all times. There should be no conventions in this regard.

Production Credits

An earlier version of *After You* premiered at the Alberta Theatre Projects'
1994 playRites Festival, under the title *Kawartha*, with the following cast:

YOUNG JEAN .... Megan Leitch
YOUNG ADELE .... Gina Wilkinson
JEAN .... Anne McGrath
ADELE .... Joyce Campion
PAUL/JEFFREY .... Chris Mackie

Directed by Colin Taylor
Costume design by Carolyn Smith
Lighting design by Harry Frehner
Sound design by Allen Rae
Set design by John Dinning
Stage Manager: Colin McCracken

Acknowledgements

The playwright gratefully acknowledges the assistance of Alberta Theatre
Projects, Candace Burley, Canadian Stage Company, Margaret Carley,
Michael Dobbin, Peter Hinton, Christine Johnston, Charlotte Lee, Megan
Leitch, Daniel Libman, Anne McGrath, Patricia Ney, Barbara Reese,
David Storch, Colin Taylor, Iris Turcott, Bob White, and Gina Wilkinson.

Dave Carley

Dave Carley's plays have been produced across Canada and the United States, and in Japan. *Writing With Our Feet* was nominated for the 1992 Governor General's Award and *Taking Liberties* was a nominee for the 1992 Chalmers Award. Dave has also written extensively for radio, and works as a script editor for the CBC Radio drama program, *Stereodrama*.

ACT ONE

(It is Sunday night of Labour Day weekend, the last weekend of summer. It is night. JEAN is standing on a rock, near water's edge. She is wearing robes of generic ecclesiastical persuasion, distinguished only by strips of imitation Native symbols, woven down the front.

YOUNG ADELE and YOUNG JEAN become visible, standing behind JEAN. They are dressed in light summer wear, 1938-vintage. Then, in dimmer light: ADELE. She is lying on an old chaise lounge. She looks out to water. JEAN raises her arms.)

JEAN: We are close now. Very close to God. He is as near to us as the thick waters of this lake, as near as...as near as...damn.

YOUNG JEAN: As near as the granite...

JEAN: ...the granite these waters rub, as near as whatever that pine is supposed to be doing.

YOUNG ADELE: Buckling.

YOUNG JEAN: Where's your brain!

JEAN: How the hell am I supposed to remember "buckling"? What the hell is a "buckling pine".

YOUNG ADELE: It's an image. It's all alone, it's bending from the wind, buckling but unbowed.

YOUNG JEAN: She knows. She's just embarrassed she can't remember.

JEAN: God is very close. You need only turn your faces, lift your faces, raise your faces…

YOUNG ADELE: Arms

JEAN: Raise your goddamn arms, reach up, reach up…

YOUNG ADELE: Reach through the dazzled skies…

YOUNG JEAN: Through the scatterings of stars…

> *(ADELE is becoming restless in her bed. She murmurs PAUL's name.)*

JEAN: Reach across the trackless miles, reach past the scatterings of stars and planets, turn your face to Him. OK, now I'm cooking. Turn your faces to Him, stare through the heat of memory and the nearing frost…

YOUNG JEAN: Through ancient hurt…

YOUNG ADELE: And thwarted dreams…

JEAN: Through approaching sorrow.

> *(PAUL has begun moving out of the lake. He is naked. He is coming into the vision of JEAN, YOUNG JEAN and YOUNG ADELE.)*

Lift up your head and your heart and taste his warm perfect breath, lift your face, let him brush a kiss across your soul.

> *(PAUL is now completely in their vision.)*

Oh my God.

> *(YOUNG ADELE and YOUNG JEAN murmur this under, as well. The three women are frozen. PAUL continues walking towards them. They*

seem to inhale deeply. PAUL walks by them. They exhale. PAUL walks to ADELE; she is still murmering his name. She sees him, reaches up to him. PAUL leans down over her and gently brushes back her hair. He then kisses her long on the lips. ADELE lies back, her eyes closing. She is dying.

The other three women are watching this with absolute intensity. PAUL crouches at the side of ADELE, kisses her again on the lips, then kisses her with growing passion. There is some kind of response from the other three watching; a long sigh of envy, perhaps.

Focus back on ADELE and PAUL. PAUL will slip off.

Focus back on JEAN, YOUNG JEAN and YOUNG ADELE. JEAN has raised a pair of scissors; the other two appear to be trying to restrain her.)

YOUNG ADELE: Jean, don't!

YOUNG JEAN: You're not thinking!

(JEAN stabs scissors into her robes and begins hacking at the Native motifs.)

We've always worn that!

JEAN: Since when did you care about tradition!

YOUNG ADELE: They're beautiful!

YOUNG JEAN: It's just decoration!

JEAN: Not to some people.

YOUNG JEAN: Then some people don't have enough to think about.

JEAN: If a symbol oppresses, rip it out.

YOUNG JEAN: Who could Mary Copeland's appliqué oppress?

YOUNG ADELE: Except aesthetically!

YOUNG JEAN: There hasn't been an Indian in that church since it was built!

JEAN: That's not the point! And you don't say "Indian" anymore.

YOUNG ADELE: What do you say?

JEAN: You say...well...I can't remember. But it's not "Indian". That's for people from India. But you don't call them Indians either.

YOUNG JEAN: *(Smelling robes)* Whew...you're going to drive them out of there like the Jews from Egypt.

YOUNG ADELE: Can she still say Jews?

JEAN: It depends on the usage.

YOUNG JEAN: How?

JEAN: It can be seen as a pejorative when.... You're trying to distract me.

YOUNG JEAN: You better air them out. Here.

(YOUNG JEAN helps JEAN out of the robes.)

You've still got two hours before you have to wear them...we'll hang them up.

JEAN: You're hoping I'll forget. I won't.

(Focus back on ADELE. She is coming out of her sleep. She is not entirely comfortable.)

ADELE: *(Murmuring.)* Paul.

YOUNG JEAN: She's so old.

JEAN: Look at me!

YOUNG JEAN: You know what I mean.

                    *(JEAN is going over to ADELE. YOUNG JEAN
                    holds up robes.)*

YOUNG ADELE: No, she won't forget.

                    *(YOUNG ADELE and YOUNG JEAN laugh,
                    move off a bit. JEAN has gone to ADELE. She
                    straightens her blanket, touches her face.
                    ADELE reaches up to her. The gesture recalls
                    her initial caress of PAUL.)*

JEAN: You're finally awake?

ADELE: My eyes are open.

JEAN: That isn't always proof with you.

                    *(YOUNG ADELE is moving over to ADELE's
                    side. YOUNG JEAN can slip away.)*

ADELE: I was dreaming.

JEAN: I heard you…you were groaning away…

YOUNG ADELE: Like Hiatus rubbing the dock.

JEAN: Like you had a goddamn toothache. Who were you
                    dreaming of?

ADELE: Can't remember. *(To YOUNG ADELE.)* She knows.

YOUNG ADELE: She doesn't have a clue.

JEAN: Eh?

ADELE: *(To YOUNG ADELE.)* Look in her eyes.

JEAN: I could probably guess.

ADELE: I think it was less who, and more what. *(Beat.)* What a what.

JEAN: Oh.

ADELE: *(To YOUNG ADELE.)* She doesn't miss much; you be careful.

YOUNG ADELE: She's too caught up with her boats.

JEAN: Juice or tea?

ADELE: What's mixed?

JEAN: Juice.

ADELE: Tea.

YOUNG ADELE: *(Swats her.)* Tell her about tonight.

ADELE: What about tonight?

YOUNG ADELE: You're not going.

ADELE: Of course I'm not going.

YOUNG ADELE: Tell her, dummy.

ADELE: I'm not going tonight.

JEAN: Of course you're not going.

ADELE: *(To YOUNG ADELE.)* She already knew. Dummy.

(YOUNG JEAN has reappeared.)

YOUNG JEAN: Not going where?

YOUNG ADELE: To the end-of-summer service.

ADELE: The water might be rough.

YOUNG JEAN: Wait a minute…we've never missed.

ADELE: I can't sit on those pews that long.

JEAN: No one's expecting you to.

YOUNG JEAN: Everyone will wonder. They're talking as it is. They want to know why Paul left so suddenly and why you're holed up on your island. It's just the parade over, then a one hour...

YOUNG ADELE: I want this summer to end!

YOUNG JEAN: Nothing's quite that easy! You got us into this! I'll get us out! That means I call the shots. Addie, even Archie's asking questions, and if he's suspicious...

ADELE: I can never remember who anyone is. They hide under those tans and dark glasses.

JEAN: They've brought back the boat parade. Haven't had it since the war and now some Yank over on the narrows thinks we should start it up again.

ADELE: I can watch it from here.

YOUNG ADELE: They'll see it in my eyes. Women can tell.

YOUNG JEAN: Wear sunglasses. Father'll be over in the new boat in half an hour.

JEAN: I'm supposed to perch in the front of Jeffy's boat like goddamn Britannia because some carpetbagger found out I'm the oldest person on the lake. They love history. Makes sense; they write it. And they expect me to give a benediction. From memory! Because someone told the goddamn Yank I'm ordained.

YOUNG ADELE: I really don't think they're called "Yanks" anymore.

JEAN: What was I getting you? Juice. *(Checks watch.)* Yes, juice.

ADELE: It's making me sleepy.

JEAN: It's supposed to.

ADELE: I want to see the parade. Does it have to be every half hour?

(JEAN has exited. ADELE is left alone, with YOUNG JEAN and YOUNG ADELE nearby.

> *YOUNG JEAN comes over to YOUNG ADELE,*
> *who is looking with binoculars into the near*
> *distance. ADELE watches from her bed.)*

YOUNG JEAN: Where's he now?

YOUNG ADELE: Coming up to the point.

YOUNG JEAN: He'll grow fins, he's been swimming so much.

YOUNG ADELE: Tiny little fins to match his tiny little horns.

> *(YOUNG JEAN swats her.)*

                         You like him.

ADELE: So you back off.

YOUNG ADELE: *(To ADELE.)* Shut up.

YOUNG JEAN: *(To YOUNG ADELE.)* Shut up.

ADELE: *(To YOUNG ADELE.)* Shut up?

YOUNG ADELE: *(To YOUNG JEAN.)* A tender spot?

YOUNG JEAN: No.

ADELE: She found him. She dragged him up here. Ergo he's
                         hers.

YOUNG ADELE: Stay out of this. *(To YOUNG JEAN.)* How come you
                         won't talk about him then?

YOUNG JEAN: Nothing to say.

YOUNG ADELE: I don't believe you.

ADELE: Oh...quit fishing.

YOUNG JEAN: There's nothing between Paul and me. Never was.
                         Never will be. There especially won't be if anyone
                         ever thinks I think there ever might be, which there
                         won't be.

YOUNG ADELE: Why not?

YOUNG JEAN: It's a cruel and unjust world.

YOUNG ADELE: You're mad about him.

ADELE: Finders keepers.

> *(YOUNG ADELE puts a pillow over ADELE's face. She pushes it off.)*

Tramp.

> *(YOUNG ADELE puts the pillow back. From under.)*

Town pump.

YOUNG JEAN: I respect him, he respects me. *(Straightening up ADELE.)* He's nice.

YOUNG ADELE: *(Rolling her eyes at ADELE, who also makes a face, despite herself.)* He's nice.

> *(ADELE and YOUNG ADELE laugh.)*

YOUNG JEAN: What's wrong with that!

YOUNG ADELE: Nothing! It's very—

ADELE: Nice. *(Shudders.)*

YOUNG JEAN: Sure it would be...nice

ADELE: Nice to what?

YOUNG JEAN: OK. It would nice to have a boyfriend. Other than Archie Copeland. But it's not going to happen. Not in this lifetime. And I'm not wasting my time wishing for things that won't happen. *(Reaching for binoculars.)* But I can look.

YOUNG ADELE: Anyway, he's too much like your father.

YOUNG JEAN: What!

YOUNG ADELE: It's a common manifestation of the female psyche.

ADELE: What do they say about "a little learning..."?

YOUNG JEAN: You're crazy!

YOUNG ADELE: It's psychology. That's right up your alley. It's very nearly a science. Some women are attracted to father figures. You, for example. You like Paul because he's exactly like your father.

YOUNG JEAN: He's not!

YOUNG ADELE: Plug full of ideology, driven. OK, so the ideology is the polar opposite to your father's, the impulse is the same. Look at him thrashing about our lake like...like an overmotivated pickerel!

YOUNG JEAN: *(Puts down binoculars.)* He's cleared the point.

YOUNG ADELE: So does he dance?

YOUNG JEAN: Of course he dances. I think he dances. How would I know?

                (YOUNG JEAN is moving off.)

ADELE: He's a wonderful dancer. One of the best in the world. Which you'll soon discover. Now come here.

                (YOUNG ADELE comes and sits with ADELE. YOUNG JEAN is off.)

                You're a real little bitch, aren't you.

YOUNG ADELE: I'm romantic.

ADELE: A real little romantic bitch.

YOUNG ADELE: Any complaints?

ADELE: Your skin is so soft. And your hair…it's so thick.

YOUNG ADELE: It gets me by.

ADELE: It'll get us by so much. Literary derision.

YOUNG ADELE: Envy, exile…

ADELE: Wars.

YOUNG ADELE: There's that word again.

ADELE: Wars?

YOUNG ADELE: Jean says there's one coming.

ADELE: There's always one coming. To be young and beautiful again, for five minutes even. I could spout some blank verse, we could drink…what?

YOUNG ADELE: Martinis.

ADELE: No, it was something French. Doesn't matter. Whatever it was, I'd down it, then I'd take them home, to bed.

YOUNG ADELE: Who? *(As ADELE shrugs.)* Name them.

ADELE: Got a phone book?

(ADELE and YOUNG ADELE laugh.)

It's a blur of huffing hormones now. But I gave it all up when I turned sixty. Same year as Jean got ordained. She found God, I turned celibate. Jean called it divine synchronicity. But for me—it was just a rapid decline in opportunity.

(JEAN has arrived with another drink.)

JEAN: Here.

(*ADELE makes a negative response.*)

It tastes fine.

ADELE: Too sweet. Too much sugar.

JEAN: I'll try again. And I'll start dinner. We're having it early.

ADELE: Why?

JEAN: What've we been talking about! It's the end of summer service at St. Pete's, I'm being hauled out of mothballs for the historical edification of some Yank, and I have to stand in the front of the lead boat like a (*Sniffs.*) stinky relic.

(*YOUNG ADELE is wrapping up ADELE.*)

ADELE: I don't want to miss the boat parade. But how are you getting there...you paddling?

(*YOUNG JEAN is visible, off to one side.*)

YOUNG ADELE: We paddling to the dance...or is he swimming, too?

YOUNG JEAN: Father's lending us Hiatus.

(*JEAN is moving off, holding her robes.*)

JEAN: Jeffrey's taking me.

ADELE: In that awful boat! Where's Hiatus!

JEAN: Hiatus sank!

ADELE: Sank!

JEAN: In the back channel. With dignity. In 1938. 1 sank it.

YOUNG ADELE: Settling into the thick water...

ADELE: It's not such a bad way to go.

JEAN: Tell that to Hiatus.

(JEAN is going in, with YOUNG JEAN.)

I'm still taking these abominations off.

YOUNG JEAN: I can't believe you went religious on me. Sometimes when you're up there sermonizing I want to choke at the absurdity of it all.

JEAN: *(Going in.)* You atheists are so delicate.

YOUNG JEAN: Where did I go wrong?

(JEAN and YOUNG JEAN are off. PAUL has entered. He wraps his arms around YOUNG ADELE, who is standing close to ADELE. ADELE is plainly distracted.)

ADELE: That awful thing of Jeffrey's. It's like a rocket.

YOUNG ADELE: It shakes the lake.

PAUl: We shake the lake.

ADELE: You can't see over the front and if you look sideways everything's a blur. You want to barf. I'd be terrified to ride in it.

PAUL: You don't have a timid bone in your body.

ADELE: I do now. It scares the wits out of me just looking at it.

YOUNG ADELE: How do you think you got over here in June?

ADELE: Hiatus?

YOUNG ADELE: Jeffrey brought you in his rocket. You sat up all the way from the marina, your face to the wind, crowing with joy.

ADELE: I was screaming in terror! It's not even wood...it's

	fibreglass or some such thing! Daddy's rolling in his grave.
PAUL:	It's decadent.
ADELE:	You'd know.
PAUL:	All that polish and spit just for a couple of month's joy-riding.
YOUNG ADELE:	Does everything have to have a purpose?
PAUL:	Your cousin would never ask that.
YOUNG ADELE:	Jean's not here. And I think decadent is always good.
ADELE:	"Within limits."
YOUNG ADELE:	No limits.
ADELE:	Big talk.

(JEAN and YOUNG JEAN are coming on scene. PAUL fades off.)

JEAN:	*(Returning with a drink.)* I always thought I would pay someone to exhume Hiatus. Give it to Jeffrey. But I doubt his girlfriends would like it though, and Jeffy doesn't seem interested in the old boats. So I've left it there, sunk. And to tell you the truth, I can't remember exactly where in the channel it is. It'll be there for eternity now.
ADELE:	It's a shame to lose that boat. It was the pride of a proud company.
JEAN:	As I recall, you thought Kawartha Canoe was stupid.
ADELE:	I never thought it was stupid! I said you were stupid!
JEAN:	That's right. For wanting to run it.
ADELE:	For giving it away!
YOUNG ADELE:	It's our birthright!

ADELE: Five pathetic years as a worker's co-op—the proudest boat company in the Dominion down the toilet.

YOUNG ADELE: Our grandfather and our fathers built that company.

ADELE: Yes, they were builders then. Not appeasers. Not guilty liberals, not our fathers.

JEAN: They were just the same as us. Minus the goddamn hindsight.

YOUNG ADELE: And now you're turning it over to a bunch of uneducated, unmotivated...

ADELE: Five years...that's got to be a record.

JEAN: Yes, well, we all commit acts of less than perfect rationality. Which my cousin catches in her rear-view mirror.

ADELE: I said so at the time!

YOUNG ADELE: You're stupid!

ADELE: See.

YOUNG ADELE: You're a fool! They'll destroy the place!

ADELE: OK, OK.

YOUNG JEAN: *(Going off.)* I'm a fool!

ADELE: Now you've got her going.

YOUNG JEAN: How dare you say I'm the fool! You sit there and call me a fool! GO TO HELL!

> *(YOUNG JEAN exits sharply. PAUL has come forward a bit.)*

JEAN: Wow.

PAUL: I better go after her.

YOUNG ADELE: She'll be back out. It's my cottage. Five four three two one

JEAN:	*(With her.)* three, two one
ADELE:	*(With them.)* two, one
YOUNG JEAN:	*(Storms back out.)* You can both go to hell! You have no vision! I can do it on my own!

(Storms off to applause from JEAN. PAUL is making to follow YOUNG JEAN.)

YOUNG ADELE:	Stay.
PAUL:	I better not.

(PAUL follows YOUNG JEAN partly off. She is still yelling "Go to hell" from a distance.)

JEAN:	One day Jeffy will become proud of the boats we made, and he'll sell his fibreglass horror. He'll restore himself a wood launch, like Hiatus if it wasn't in Davey Jones' locker. Next summer the Yank can have a real boat leading the parade. Children will wave. Flags'll dip.
ADELE:	Pigs will fly in chubby flocks. *(Sigh.)* We were the most beautiful girls on the lake.
JEAN:	Bah. I had the best boat, that's all.
YOUNG ADELE:	"The afternoon dazzle."
ADELE:	Yes, someone said that.
PAUL:	Like a field of diamonds.
ADELE:	Was it one of the dreadful Copelands?
JEAN:	I married a Copeland!
ADELE:	No, far too clever for a Copeland. Especially your husband Archie. The big splash at the shallow end of the gene pool. No, someone else said it.

(PAUL is pulling YOUNG ADELE into the cottage.)

PAUL: You dazzle me.

ADELE: People said things like that, then.

JEAN: Out of dimestore novels.

ADELE: At least they said it.

JEAN: They never meant it. At least Archie would've meant it.

ADELE: He was too stupid to lie. Oh, I had a certain licentious charm, and you had hair like rapids, wild black rapids. Until you went to university and got that godawful cut. During your Trotsky phase.

JEAN: I was never a Trot.

ADELE: You were something serious.

JEAN: I wasn't a Trot.

(Laughter inside from PAUL and YOUNG ADELE.)

Finish your drink.

(JEAN goes to one side, takes robes down from where they've been airing out. She begins taking off the Native motifs. ADELE lies back. They mostly watch the next scene. YOUNG JEAN and YOUNG ADELE burst back on, and are embracing, enjoying their reunion.)

YOUNG ADELE: Welcome back, stranger!

YOUNG JEAN: Stranger, yourself!

YOUNG ADELE: You've cut your hair!

YOUNG JEAN: *(Sniffing.)* What's this?

YOUNG ADELE: *Evening in Paree.*

YOUNG JEAN: You look so...sophisticated.

YOUNG ADELE: And you look so...intelligent. All that short hair. Archie will be devastated.

YOUNG JEAN: To hell with Archie. God, ten months! Feels like a decade!

YOUNG ADELE: You never wrote.

YOUNG JEAN: Every week!

YOUNG ADELE: Political diatribes don't count!

YOUNG JEAN: Reasoned arguments, but you, poetry that doesn't rhyme?

YOUNG ADELE: *(Laughing.)* Burn it. I'm moving on to prose.

> *(YOUNG ADELE and YOUNG JEAN are laughing. YOUNG ADELE looks up and sees PAUL, who has entered, and who has been standing off to one side, watching the cousins' reunion. ADELE has heaved herself to a sitting position, and sees.)*

ADELE: Oh.

YOUNG ADELE: Oh!

ADELE: Paul.

YOUNG JEAN: Addie, Paul Sloan. My cousin, Adele Findlay, the first, the only.

PAUL: *(Shaking hands.)* Hello.

YOUNG JEAN: Paul's staying with us, on Findlay West.

YOUNG ADELE: He's staying on your island.

YOUNG JEAN: This is Adele's family's island. Findlay East.

PAUL: *(Releasing YOUNG ADELE's hand.)* Jean's told me about you.

YOUNG ADELE: *(Recovering.)* How much?

YOUNG JEAN: All!

YOUNG ADELE: Well, whatever she told you, I'm sure it was accurate.

PAUL: Could it be otherwise?

YOUNG ADELE: A month ago I might have called Jean predictable. But she's cut her hair and brought you, neither of which was predictable. So now, she's only accurate.

ADELE: Already you're starting.

YOUNG ADELE: Am not!

ADELE: Then go inside. Right now. Go. Shoo.

YOUNG ADELE: Not on your life. *(To others.)* Time is not predictable, but a clock is accurate. Jean's a regular Big Ben. It's from her father. My father says you should never let facts get in the way of a good story. Jean's father believes in a liberal God, the conservative use of nails, and accuracy.

PAUL: My father believed in repetition and volume.

YOUNG ADELE: Most men do.

(JEAN is watching.)

ADELE: *(To YOUNG JEAN.)* For the love of God, say something!

YOUNG JEAN: Paul's got three papers to complete, for his degree.

ADELE: Something soft!

YOUNG JEAN: Huh?

ADELE: Be coy.

YOUNG JEAN: Coy? Uh…. This is the perfect place to concentrate on essays.

(ADELE groans.)

PAUL: I live in a boarding house...it's very noisy.

YOUNG JEAN: It's right on Dundas and the streetcars...it just made sense. I'm going to borrow a typewriter from the factory.

YOUNG ADELE: Oh that's nice. Underwoods clattering across the channel. Uh-hmm. The rap of keys, the slam of returning carriages. Lake Kawartha...home of loons and stenography. *(To PAUL.)* Might my cousin and I have a word?

YOUNG JEAN: Paul...I...uh...left Addie's present in the canoe.

PAUL: Sure, sure. I'll get it.

> *(PAUL exits. YOUNG ADELE and YOUNG JEAN watch him go, then square off. JEAN has gone back in; ADELE watches the fight.)*

YOUNG ADELE: Who is he!

YOUNG JEAN: He's a friend. What was all that? The slam of typewriters?

YOUNG ADELE: He's here until August?

YOUNG JEAN: Yes.

YOUNG ADELE: The whole summer!

YOUNG JEAN: He'll be studying all day!

YOUNG ADELE: *(Realizing.)* He's the Trotskyite! He's the one you're always on about in your letters!

YOUNG JEAN: I thought you didn't read them.

YOUNG ADELE: I can hardly wait to hear what everyone says.

YOUNG JEAN: I don't give a shit what they say.

YOUNG ADELE: Ooh...she swears now.

(YOUNG ADELE is leaving, heading towards the cottage.)

YOUNG JEAN: Where are you going!

YOUNG ADELE: I'm getting a drink. One of us swears, one of us drinks.

YOUNG JEAN: May I get something for Paul?

(YOUNG ADELE and YOUNG JEAN are exiting.)

He is my guest, after all.

YOUNG ADELE: *(Going off.)* We don't want to treat him like "shit".

(YOUNG ADELE and YOUNG JEAN move off. ADELE is sitting up, alone. She looks around. PAUL enters, carrying a parcel.)

PAUL: Where'd they go?

ADELE: That way. But it's ugly.

PAUL: Jean warned me she wouldn't want me here. She doesn't like change.

ADELE: She's just going through the motions. The groin'll kick in any minute. So come here prairie boy, come take a load off.

(PAUL sits beside ADELE.)

There. This is nice. It's not often so quiet around here. Jean's been fussing about all summer like a bug on a screen. I had a little stroke this spring. Well, three of them. Jean and her boy Tom, well, he's a man now, I guess he must be…50 or 55 or 60; Jean and Tom had to come down to Montreal and rescue me. And a few other things have gone on the fritz. So she's looking after me; but actually she's in worse shape than I am. I can't move but she's rotting away. It's a terrible thing. You should be able to assign illness. By proxy. I could take it all on and she could hang about these islands for another decade. Where are my manners! You thirsty after your trip?

PAUL: A bit.

ADELE: Try a sip of this.

(PAUL tries ADELE's drink, makes face.)

PAUL: Phew!

ADELE: Bad huh.

PAUL: It's so bitter.

ADELE: Seconal. Listen. If you and Jean aren't Trots, and you aren't a Bolshie…

PAUL: How do you know I'm not?

ADELE: Too good-looking. Only thing I know about politics, the further right you go, the handsomer the men. Jean always hated that theory. You're the exception that proves the rule. So what are you exactly. Just an ordinary garden variety Socialist?

PAUL: Yeah. Sorry.

ADELE: Any seven year plans up your sleeve?

PAUL: Oh, just change the world.

ADELE: Starting with banging Miss Addie?

PAUL: It's a beginning. You liberate the libido, you liberate nations. It's all the same revolution.

ADELE: That's socialism?

PAUL: As I practise it.

ADELE: Well I'll be damned. I spent fifty years voting for the wrong party. But listen prairie boy, if sex is so important to the revolution, why aren't you sleeping with Jean?

PAUL: Maybe I am.

ADELE: Can't fool me. She's desperate for liberation but it's me you're sizing up for invasion.

PAUL: Would that be so bad?

ADELE: What's one more army? (*Touching PAUL.*) When I first saw you...

PAUL: You threw a tantrum, as I recall.

ADELE: That was to cover up...

PAUL: I know.

ADELE: I'm that transparent?

PAUL: Yes.

ADELE: Do you remember my skin?

(PAUL is touching her.)

No...before.

PAUL: Yes.

ADELE: Because I haven't forgotten yours.

(PAUL is taking off his shirt for her.)

It's exactly as I remember.

PAUL: Your hair spreads over the rock.

ADELE: We swim the back channel, where no one comes.

PAUL: Like Adam and Eve.

ADELE: Another couple on the road to nowhere.

PAUL: But we don't care.

ADELE: We don't dare.

> *(The other three emerge. YOUNG JEAN has two*
> *bottles of beer, one of which she hands to PAUL.*
> *YOUNG ADELE has a drink, probably gin, and a*
> *smaller parcel. JEAN has a drink for ADELE.)*

YOUNG ADELE: He can keep Archie Copeland at bay.

YOUNG JEAN: *(To PAUL.)* Hear that? You're on guard duty!

> *(PAUL is crossing over to them.)*

JEAN: Why are you sitting up!

ADELE: I wanted to see over to the back channel.

PAUL: *(Holding up parcel.)* It got a little wet in the boat.

YOUNG ADELE: Hiatus is leaking.

JEAN: That's really bright. You'll topple off the porch and
                   sink in the drink with Hiatus.

ADELE: Wouldn't be such a bad way to go.

> *(PAUL hands parcel to YOUNG ADELE.)*

YOUNG JEAN: You won't like it.

> *(YOUNG ADELE hands YOUNG JEAN her*
> *parcel. JEAN is making ADELE lie back.)*

YOUNG ADELE: You'll hate this.

JEAN: Back you go. And here's your drink.

ADELE: Forget rolling into the Back Channel. I'm going to wash away in a torrent of pee.

JEAN: It has to be every half hour.

> *(PAUL, YOUNG ADELE and YOUNG JEAN have raised their glasses. ADELE does the same. JEAN doesn't have a drink, but will put her hand out to steady her ADELE's.)*

YOUNG JEAN: To summer...

PAUL: To summer...

YOUNG ADELE: Summer...

ADELE: Down the sewer.

> *(YOUNG ADELE and YOUNG JEAN begin opening their presents.)*

YOUNG ADELE: Too soft for political tracts.

YOUNG JEAN: *(Opening hers; ironic.)* A McGill scarf?

YOUNG ADELE: For those cold picket lines. *(Opens hers; it's a University of Toronto sweater, the same one that ADELE has draped over herself.)* Oh, a U of T jersey.

PAUL: For those bitter days window-shopping on Ste Catherine.

> *(Awkward pause.)*

YOUNG JEAN: Did you see along the shoreline?

PAUL: It's beautiful.

YOUNG JEAN: Adele writes about it.

YOUNG ADELE: Drop dead.

YOUNG JEAN: Fiction. About the animals.

YOUNG ADELE: Shut up.

PAUL: I'd like to read it.

YOUNG ADELE: You won't get the chance. I'm developing a style. It's not there yet.

YOUNG JEAN: She's very good. She'll be published some day. The book's a...damn, what's the word?

YOUNG ADELE: Allegory. Now shut up.

YOUNG JEAN: The animals stand in for humans and have adventures...it's set right here! There's a passage where a great blue heron falls from the sky right on that rock and

YOUNG ADELE: Jean!

(Another awkward pause.)

                Anyway, I'm new to fiction. Mostly I've written poetry.

PAUL: I know! Jean's showed me some.

YOUNG JEAN: Oh oh.

YOUNG ADELE: She did.

PAUL: Why can't it rhyme?

YOUNG ADELE: Not everything is written for chanting.

                        (Light down on YOUNG ADELE, PAUL and YOUNG JEAN. PAUL will move off, perhaps "watched off" by JEAN with her binoculars. Focus more strongly now on ADELE and JEAN. The latter has produced binoculars.)

ADELE: Let me look.

JEAN: I'm focusing. There.

ADELE: *(Looking.)* The Dobsons have their winter battens up. *(Scanning with her binoculars.)* Is that Tom sweeping the dock at St Peter's?

JEAN: Probably.

ADELE: He looks ancient.

JEAN: He'll be 55 next March.

ADELE: Couldn't be.

JEAN: Add it up. He was born in 39, you were 22.

ADELE: I was 21. What the hell year is this? Never mind. I don't want to know. *(Still looking.)* There's something flying back and forth. *(Checks front of binoculars, then looks out again.)* Like a silverfish. Here.

> *(YOUNG ADELE and YOUNG JEAN have one pair of binoculars between them; it's a bit of a wrestling match.)*

YOUNG ADELE: *(Looking.)* Back and forth, back and forth.

JEAN: *(Looking.)* That's our Jerry. He says his boat's the fastest on the lake.

YOUNG JEAN: *(Taking binoculars.)* Paul's under tremendous pressure to get his year. His scholarships are hanging in the balance.

> *(ADELE has stopped watching the lake now, and is watching PAUL swim; her binoculars will follow movements of YOUNG ADELE and YOUNG JEAN.)*

ADELE: *(Looking.)* Back and forth, back and forth.

JEAN: You'd think he'd find it monotonous.

ADELE: *(Looking.)* So powerful.

JEAN: He's too young for such a big boat.

                 (JEAN checks her watch.)

                 Every fifteen minutes now.

                 *(JEAN exits with empty glass. YOUNG JEAN and
                 YOUNG ADELE are watching PAUL; ADELE
                 does for a while, then lies back and dozes off.)*

YOUNG ADELE: Why didn't he get his year in May, like everyone
                 else?

YOUNG JEAN: Too busy.

YOUNG ADELE: With you?

YOUNG JEAN: No. Spain.

YOUNG ADELE: *(Mock heroic.)* Spain.

YOUNG JEAN: Christ Addie, would you grow up!

YOUNG ADELE: What'd I do! I say, "Spain" and you jump down my
                 throat!

YOUNG JEAN: I'm sick of your digs! You know, if you'd read a
                 newspaper you might find it helps your goddamn
                 poetry. You want to write about...pine cones
                 and...goddamn herons with broken wings...fine, go
                 corner the market. I'm not going to condemn you but
                 don't stand there saying "Spain", like he's...like
                 we're misguided fools because it's wrong, it's wrong
                 to mock.

YOUNG ADELE: I'm not mocking!

YOUNG JEAN: You are! You always are!

YOUNG ADELE: It's just me, it's a charming idiosyncrasy.

YOUNG JEAN: It's arrogant and it's just too damn easy.

YOUNG ADELE: We weren't all born bleeding for the world.

YOUNG JEAN: We were born the same. We've made different choices.

YOUNG ADELE: Your choice is better of course.

YOUNG JEAN: Actually, it is. You're so...so goddamn cynical. Oh...you have other words for it. "The pursuit of beauty". "The artist's life".

YOUNG ADELE: You don't understand.

YOUNG JEAN: There are artists...who are creating...who right now are writing and painting and saying things about what needs to be changed, but you're not one of them, Miss Blank Verse 1938.

YOUNG ADELE: Philistine.

YOUNG JEAN: OK, yes, I'm a Philistine! And I'm proud of it!

(YOUNG JEAN turns and starts to move off, but JEAN is coming back and catches her by the arm. They fight out of earshot of the ADELE and YOUNG ADELE.)

JEAN: So who's being evasive here?

YOUNG JEAN: I don't know what you're talking about.

JEAN: If you're going to fight her, at least be clear what you're fighting over.

YOUNG JEAN: She's a parasite!

JEAN: Uh huh.

YOUNG JEAN: Her writing's worthless!

JEAN: And what did all my diligent labour add up to?

YOUNG JEAN: More.

JEAN: I'm not so sure. But I do know what's bugging you.
                     You're mad because deep down you worry you'd
                     give it all up for him. Which would be appalling.
                     Paul's just a fork in the road. A wrenching one, but
                     nothing more.

                     *(JEAN goes off. YOUNG JEAN turns back to
                     YOUNG ADELE. She calms herself.)*

YOUNG JEAN: I'm sorry. I'm sorry about the poetry. I'm sorry I
                     showed it to Paul. It's good; I wanted to share it. I'm
                     sorry I yelled at you; you hit a nerve. I'm worn out. I
                     want to yell at the world, not you.

YOUNG ADELE: Apology accepted. As always.

YOUNG JEAN: You wonder why Paul's swimming like that; I can tell
                     you. Things are bad in Spain. Worse than bad. It's
                     over. He won't admit it, he still says he's going over,
                     still wants us to carry on, but it's finished. Mackenzie
                     King's made it illegal to volunteer, the deaths are
                     incredible, the retreats are in full swing. *(Pause.)* A
                     lot of us think this is just a dress rehearsal. There's
                     going to be a war, Addie.

YOUNG ADELE: I know this!

YOUNG JEAN: Then how can you sit back! *(Pause.)* Never mind.
                     Let's not get into it again. *(Sigh.)* Father's going to hit
                     the roof when he sees my grades. I spent more time at
                     factory gates than in class. That's a nasty little
                     paradox…me shivering there with my little shoebox,
                     begging money from the poor so we could send other
                     poor sods overseas to get killed fighting the rich. Me.
                     The boat queen of the Kawarthas. *(Pause.)* And to see
                     it all going up in smoke. And I don't even have a dress
                     for tonight.

YOUNG ADELE: You're coming?

YOUNG JEAN: Time to break old Archie's heart, eh?

YOUNG ADELE: Paul's coming?

YOUNG JEAN: He can swim over. So, the dress?

YOUNG ADELE: Take your pick. And can you bring back my cigs. I think they're on the dresser.

(YOUNG JEAN exits. YOUNG ADELE looks out to where PAUL should be, but can't locate him.)

Where is he?

ADELE: *(Stirring.)* Paul?

YOUNG ADELE: Paul?

(YOUNG ADELE is worried. She runs to the shoreline, fixes her binoculars and scans the water. ADELE is restless until PAUL appears at her side. He leans down and kisses her, then stands behind her, and rubs her shoulders etc. He has been swimming.)

ADELE: You've got to go back.

PAUL: We still have a few minutes.

ADELE: She'll be here soon. There...I'm sure I heard the whistle. Hear it? The steamer's at Dobsons'...Jean's is next!

PAUL: They've still got to cross the channel and Jean's wharf is on the far side of her island.

(ADELE pushes PAUL away.)

ADELE: Monday...it's just two days.

(PAUL kisses her again.)

No!

PAUL: Ten more minutes!

ADELE: GO!

                 (ADELE pushes PAUL away. He flies over to shoreline, coming up behind YOUNG ADELE, and startling her.)

YOUNG ADELE: Where'd you go! I lost sight

PAUL: I swam around the point to the back channel, and ran back along the path. Where's Jean?

YOUNG ADELE: Inside, picking out a dress. She'll be hours. She's such a debutante.

PAUL: *(Laughs.)* Why do I have trouble believing that? So...where's the dance?

YOUNG ADELE: Juniper. *(Handing him the binoculars.)* The island, one over from Copelands'. *(Aims his binoculars.)* See the pavilion? There's a swing band tonight. But of course you wouldn't be interested.

                 (YOUNG JEAN is watching, holding cigarettes, wearing a red dress. JEAN is also there, with juice. ADELE had been watching at the start of YOUNG ADELE and PAUL's exchange, but is dozing a bit.)

PAUL: What makes you think that?

YOUNG ADELE: Isn't dancing a bit...frivolous?

PAUL: I often get a bit...frivolous.

                 (YOUNG ADELE looks doubtful; scoffs.)

YOUNG ADELE: I bet.

PAUL: I was walking a picket line a week ago—the day before we came up here—there we were, Jean and I and a few others. We were trudging back and forth, absolutely grim, not a smile for miles. We're singing some fizzy little tune—*The Internationale*. And all of a sudden I got this urge to skip.

YOUNG ADELE: Skip.

PAUL: Honest Injun.

YOUNG ADELE: Jean'll be glad you're coming. She can show you off.

PAUL: Why would she do that?

(YOUNG JEAN starts over to them.)

JEAN: Wait.

(JEAN stops YOUNG JEAN, fixes her dress, pulling it tighter at the waist, pulling the neckline down, etc.)

I can't believe I'm doing this.

YOUNG JEAN: *(As JEAN is working, to ADELE and PAUL.)*
               So...what do you think?

PAUL: Looks great.

ADELE: *(To YOUNG ADELE.)* You can top that.

YOUNG ADELE: I better find myself something.

YOUNG JEAN: *(To JEAN, who is still industriously "adjusting".)*
               OK, OK, enough.

ADELE: The yellow one.

(YOUNG ADELE is running off, YOUNG JEAN and PAUL are exiting.)

YOUNG JEAN: We should go home and get ready.

> *(JEAN has come to ADELE. She props her up a bit, and keeps her drinking.)*

JEAN: Here.

ADELE: Isn't this too much?

JEAN: Every fifteen minutes.

ADELE: I'll start hallucinating. I already dozed off and dreamt about Paul.

> *(JEAN takes drink away.)*

JEAN: OK, we'll slow up.

ADELE: I wish I knew what happened to him. I always imagined he ended up in Africa somewhere, leading a revolutionary movement. Or running a bar for retired Trots, on the Isle of Capri. *(Laughs.)* Here I am, here we are...it's this time and I'm wondering about...him. Stupid, eh.

JEAN: Very stupid.

ADELE: The most logical thing would be he went back to Saskatchewan and joined the CCF.

JEAN: He's dead.

ADELE: Yes, that's possible. He'd be 76 or 77.

JEAN: No...he is dead. It's quite pathetic really... He fell.

ADELE: How do you know this!

JEAN: I kept in contact over the years. His...widow wrote me with the news.

ADELE: You were writing to him?

JEAN: At Christmas...to tell him...update him on Tom. He had a right to know how Tom was...growing up.

ADELE: You never told me this!

JEAN:	Why the hell would I? What would you have done...hopped the Concorde to England and broken up his marriage? He had a wife.
ADELE:	And children?
JEAN:	...Three. And grandchildren.
ADELE:	You never told me. And I met him for tea once.
ADELE:	You saw him!
JEAN:	When I was MP. The only perk I ever got in my fleeting career...a trip to England. For a goddamn conference on cod. Nowadays MPs go everywhere but all I got was one fish convention because the Minister couldn't go and someone remembered my family made boats. I snuck out of the conference and phoned Paul; he came down to London. Lunch was a disaster. Paul was teaching political thought at some new university. Political thought...now there's an oxymoron. He bragged he was a respected academic...there's another one. Said he had tenure, but he was so bitter. He was sarcastic about the boat company...said he knew I'd never make a go if it. Said the co-op model never works. Said I was nuts to go into politics, then spent an hour describing the infighting in his department. It was the longest couple of hours I'd ever spent, enduring the bleatings of this tenured old shrew with tufts of hair sprouting from his ears...
ADELE:	No!
JEAN:	And a mottled, porous nose...
ADELE:	No!
JEAN:	Obviously a drinker. I always knew Paul was a fraud, right from Day One. I knew the only revolution he was committed to was the one you do on a mattress.
ADELE:	Did he ask about me?
JEAN:	No. Yes. He'd read your book, wanted to know if you'd ever written a sequel. Then it was back to the departmental politics.

ADELE: He's dead?

JEAN: Fell. At a garden party. Tripped over a croquet hoop.

ADELE: Paul!

JEAN: Do you hate me for telling you?

ADELE: I hate when you don't tell me things. You really never told me this before?

JEAN: No.

ADELE: If I seem shocked...it's because it's nothing like I'd imagined. I could've invented much better. Skewered by Mau Maus. Strafed by Stukas. But a croquet hoop? *(Starts to laugh.)* Oh Jesus, I don't mean to laugh. A croquet hoop?

JEAN: *(Trying to stay solemn.)* Yes.

ADELE: It's so...so...

JEAN: The middle hoops.

ADELE: *(Now really laughing.)* He was off to fight the fascists.

JEAN: *(Laughing too.)* Face first, right on a goddamn ball.

ADELE: The red one!

JEAN: We shouldn't be laughing.

ADELE: Who's laughing!

JEAN: Not me.

            (ADELE laughs and then that ends. JEAN now hands ADELE her drink, stirs it. ADELE reaches for it with two hands.)

            We can only hope to go with dignity.

ADELE: Just a dash of it.

JEAN: That's the very best we can hope for.

ADELE:	Yes.
JEAN:	So drink. Drink.

(Lights down on JEAN and ADELE. Music. It's after the dance. PAUL and YOUNG ADELE are on the verandah, dancing. YOUNG JEAN is watching. They have drinks, cigarettes, are wearing their party dresses.)

PAUL:	How much proof do you need?
YOUNG ADELE:	A bit more.
PAUL:	I took lessons.
YOUNG JEAN:	When did you have time!
PAUL:	Three summers ago, when I worked at the Y.

(YOUNG JEAN cuts in.)

YOUNG JEAN:	I can't picture you in a dance class.
PAUL:	I was lonely. I'd just come to Toronto. I didn't know anyone east of Lake Superior. I was a sitting duck. I'd have done anything for a smile.
YOUNG JEAN:	I hate to think of you like that.
PAUL:	The gym was full of people just like me. A hundred lonely immigrants from small towns, stopping, starting, shuffling about with the partners we were assigned.

(YOUNG ADELE is cutting in.)

YOUNG ADELE:	May I? I'll bet there was a stampede for you.
PAUL:	I was a wallflower.
YOUNG ADELE:	No.

PAUL: Two left feet, couldn't even make conversation because I had to count off...

YOUNG ADELE: My father taught us.

PAUL: You're lucky.

(YOUNG JEAN cuts in.)

YOUNG JEAN: My turn. Why's that luck? What use is it? God! I sound like father! He won't dance; he only works.

PAUL: Which is amazing.

YOUNG JEAN: What's amazing.

PAUL: That they do. Work so much. Your dad and uncle going in to the city every Sunday night, leaving their islands to spend the week at the factory in Ashburnham...if I was your Dad...

YOUNG JEAN: You're nothing like him!

(YOUNG ADELE cuts in.)

PAUL: If I was your Dad, I'd never leave.

YOUNG ADELE: Isn't that revisionist thinking?

PAUL: Depends what I do here to fill my time.

YOUNG ADELE: I'll be the soul of discretion.

PAUL: Who was the fellow trailing her all night?

YOUNG JEAN: I can hear.

YOUNG ADELE: Weren't you introduced? That's the famous Archie Copeland.

YOUNG JEAN: Who are you talking about?

YOUNG ADELE: The great tidal bore.

YOUNG JEAN: Oh, Archie.

PAUL:	I met him. I mean, "who is he?"
YOUNG ADELE:	The Copelands have the third island over. Archie's been crazy about Jean ever since she shoved him off her dock when they were six. Daddy had to leap in and save him.
YOUNG JEAN:	I still hate him.
YOUNG ADELE:	They're fated to marry.
YOUNG JEAN:	I'll rot in hell first.
YOUNG ADELE:	And breed hundreds of little Archies.
PAUL:	If you hate him so much, why'd you spend the whole night dancing with him?

(YOUNG ADELE swings him away.)

YOUNG ADELE:	Because you were dancing with me.

(Lights back up on JEAN and ADELE. JEAN bends over ADELE, who is holding up her drink and making a face.)

ADELE:	The Hemlock Society's going to have your ass.
JEAN:	Damn. I'll add sugar.
ADELE:	You'd think they'd have a recipe.
JEAN:	They do. But it's very technical. You practically have to be a pharmacist. I'm doing my best.
ADELE:	Well something's wrong. All of a sudden I'm wider awake than I've been most of my life. Maybe I'm like Rasputin. Maybe you'll have to tie rocks to my ankles and throw me in the Back Channel.
YOUNG ADELE:	Sink her with Hiatus.
PAUL:	Drop her from the flagpole.

ADELE: Sentence me to a weekend with Archie.

JEAN: I'll get you another drink.

ADELE: Was it something I said?

> *(YOUNG ADELE and PAUL have stopped dancing, near ADELE. JEAN is going in. As she passes YOUNG JEAN she picks up a pack of cigarettes and slaps them into YOUNG JEAN's hand.)*

JEAN: You are criminally dense.

YOUNG JEAN: What's that supposed to mean?

JEAN: Don't leave them alone.

YOUNG JEAN: Who. Them? Oil and water.

> *(With a nod, JEAN indicates to YOUNG JEAN that she should take the cigarettes and gin and get over with YOUNG ADELE and PAUL. JEAN goes off and YOUNG JEAN goes over to the others.)*

                I owe you a medal.

PAUL: Me?

YOUNG JEAN: For delivering me from Archie.

YOUNG ADELE: We're somewhat starved for novelty.

PAUL: Ah...I'm a novelty.

YOUNG ADELE: It's been the same old crowd forever. Jean and I know every sweaty palm, every gust of halitosis...

YOUNG JEAN: ...Who can be trusted to be a gentleman

YOUNG ADELE: ...Who can be relied upon to grope. There's Copelands if you want to die of boredom, Dobsons if you just want to die. The Dobsons prove Darwinism.

	They should have introduced them as evidence at that trial in Kentucky.
YOUNG JEAN:	Tennessee.
YOUNG ADELE:	The Dobson brain cannot grasp machinery. They will die out any day now.
YOUNG JEAN:	Last summer Mrs D gored herself on a can opener, almost bled to death. And Bill sank their Packard on the long weekend...flew it off the bridge.
YOUNG ADELE:	"Just got bored of driving." And Ann piled their inboard up on the rocks in the back channel, nearly blew herself to Spain. She got thrown fifty feet, used the occasion to complete a perfect three point dive with a double pike. It showed style, but she landed headfirst on a log.

(YOUNG JEAN is building up to say something.)

	Right Jeannie?
YOUNG JEAN:	I have something to tell you.
PAUL:	Now?
YOUNG JEAN:	She has to know.
PAUL:	But
YOUNG ADELE:	Tell me what.
PAUL:	Why not tomorrow.
YOUNG ADELE:	What!
YOUNG JEAN:	I'm...I'm not actually going to spend summer here. I mean, I am, weekends, but otherwise, no. I went away, spent the whole winter thinking, trying to decide what I should do, with my life. Didn't really come up with any hard and fast conclusions. Did decide one thing...it's something to do with the factory.
YOUNG ADELE:	What do you mean?

YOUNG JEAN: I think building boats is just as much in the core of me,
                 it's what drives me, as much as these islands get you
                 writing. There's something at Kawartha Canoe that
                 will tie together everything I've been feeling this past
                 year. Things were happening everywhere and there I
                 am, begging nickels and dimes, like I said...taking
                 from the poor to fight the rich when in the middle of
                 Ashburnham there's this factory that my family
                 owns... I'm going to go work there.

YOUNG ADELE: To do what? Type letters. File?

YOUNG JEAN: I don't know.

YOUNG ADELE: Build boats?

YOUNG JEAN: Something.

YOUNG ADELE: How's that better than this?

YOUNG JEAN: I didn't say "better".

YOUNG ADELE: But that's the inference.

YOUNG JEAN: It's not either/or, it's just something I have to do.

YOUNG ADELE: *(To PAUL.)* Did you know about this? You probably
                 talked her into it.

PAUL: Jean came up with it!

YOUNG ADELE: *(To PAUL.)* You've got her so wound up she doesn't
                 know if she's coming or going, or why.

YOUNG JEAN: It was my decision!

YOUNG ADELE: Fine. Just fine. So much for summer. My cousin the
                 Trotskyite must be with the people, the people she
                 knows and loves so intimately, and her cousin will not
                 stand in the way of this. Fine, wreck summer, wreck
                 your summer, go to hell just go to hell.

                         *(YOUNG ADELE exits. PAUL and YOUNG
                         JEAN stare after her. JEAN has seen this and
                         ADELE is snapped awake by the yelling.)*

YOUNG JEAN:	Was I right or was I right?
PAUL:	That was even worse than we expected.
YOUNG JEAN:	She's got a wicked temper and she hates having her plans disrupted. But hold on, she'll be back. Five four three two one

(YOUNG ADELE flies back out.)

YOUNG ADELE:	This island is the preserve of the petit bourgeoisie. Workers of the world can get the fucking hell off.

(YOUNG ADELE slams back inside. Nervous laughter from the others.)

ADELE:	I never said that.
JEAN:	Yes you did.
ADELE:	You were the one who swore like a trooper. I had a more eloquent approach to language.
YOUNG JEAN:	Garbage.
ADELE:	Listen. I want this on the record. I'm nearly eighty. I'm about to cross the bar. And in all my life, in all those years, I have never once, never once said the word "Fuck".

(A long pause; some throat clearing.)

	That doesn't count. That was the Seconal talking.
YOUNG JEAN:	*(To PAUL.)* We may as well go back to my island.
ADELE:	It felt good though.
PAUL:	When's your steamer?
JEAN:	I'm sure it did.

ADELE:	Throw a couple of fucks in your benediction tonight.
YOUNG JEAN:	Six pm tomorrow. *(Looks at watch.)* Tonight.
PAUL:	We'd better go then.

(PAUL heads for dock.)

YOUNG JEAN:	Paul?

(JEAN and ADELE are watching this. PAUL stops.)

PAUL:	Yes?
YOUNG JEAN:	Nothing.
PAUL:	What.
YOUNG JEAN:	Never mind.
· PAUL:	What.
YOUNG JEAN:	It's just that…in twenty summers…Addie and I…we've never fought. So far this summer, we've done nothing but.
JEAN:	Keep going.

(YOUNG JEAN seems to be at a loss.)

You could use some… *(Groping for the word.)*

ADELE:	Comfort.
YOUNG JEAN:	I can't say that.
ADELE:	Try.
YOUNG JEAN:	*(To PAUL.)* And well…there's this…I don't know how to say this…I could, uh, use some…

PAUL: Comfort?

(Pause.)

ADELE: For God's sake, give the poor thing a hug!

JEAN: Don't patronise me! He'll hug me; he doesn't need you telling him.

(PAUL has put his arms out. To ADELE.)

See.

(YOUNG JEAN at first almost seems not to understand, and JEAN has to give her a little push. PAUL puts his arms around YOUNG JEAN, his intent apparently to comfort. YOUNG JEAN awkwardly puts her arms around him. JEAN has picked up her scissors.)

PAUL: It's no good fighting.

YOUNG JEAN: We want such different things.

PAUL: The whole world's fighting, maybe it has to be the same here.

(PAUL and YOUNG JEAN stand there for a moment. Then YOUNG JEAN lifts her head, as if expecting a kiss, which might seem the inevitable outcome of such an embrace, in that situation, so late at night. And then PAUL does kiss her; a highly ambiguous kiss. It's a kiss that has a definite beginning and end, a formal structure and a different meaning for both participants. After the kiss, YOUNG JEAN looks down, collects herself, looks back up and smiles, then winks at JEAN.)

YOUNG JEAN: Race you to the boat!

JEAN: Damn!

                *(PAUL and YOUNG JEAN race off; PAUL
                exiting completely and YOUNG JEAN stopping
                near JEAN. JEAN stabs her scissors into the
                vestments.)*

                Off they go!

ADELE: Archie's sister spent two summer "creating" those!
                It's the only remotely interesting thing Mary ever did!

YOUNG JEAN: It's the only remotely interesting thing you've ever
                worn!

JEAN: I thought you hated me being clergy!

YOUNG JEAN: *(Caught.)* Aesthetically.

JEAN: *(To ADELE.)* So where do you suppose Mary
                Copeland got the design?

ADELE: Out of her feeble head.

JEAN: Exactly!

                (JEAN continues tearing off the panels.)

ADELE: Jean!

YOUNG JEAN: She read a book on "native lore". Well, maybe not
                "read". Not Mary. But she looked at the pictures
                intently.

JEAN: They're not authentic! And they shouldn't be on
                robes used in a Christian service.

YOUNG JEAN: Indians can be Christians!

JEAN: That's not the point.

ADELE: What is the point?

JEAN: I'm not going over to St. Peter's to bless a bunch of goddamn Yankees when I'm wearing a lot of pseudo-aboriginal hoohaw whipped up by some IQ-challenged Copeland. It's politically incorrect.

(YOUNG JEAN and ADELE stare at JEAN.)

ADELE &
YOUNG JEAN: Huh/What?

JEAN: To think that I preached in that church for fifteen summers wearing these abominations.

YOUNG JEAN: You're mad!

JEAN: I may be seventy-five...

ADELE: Eighty.

JEAN: *(Over.)* And falling apart at the seams but I'm not too old to see the light.

ADELE: Mary Copeland will be so upset.

JEAN: Mary's dead, goddamn it! She's been dead for years! Everyone's dead!

ADELE: Archie's dead?

JEAN: Extremely dead!

ADELE: You're sure.

JEAN: Positive.

YOUNG JEAN: She dumped his ashes off the wharf.

ADELE: Because sometimes it was hard to tell with Archie. I'd see him on your verandah, just sitting there, hour after hour, and I'd think, "Oh God, Arch has finally bitten it." And then you'd fire up the barbeque and he'd open one eye. And somewhere on the lake someone'd rattle an ice cube tray. He'd open the other one. And I'd give a big sigh of relief: "Archie's made another Happy Hour."

JEAN: He meant well.

ADELE: You pushed him out of Hiatus when you were eight
                  and he never stopped loving you.

JEAN: We were ten and it was the wharf at Juniper.

YOUNG JEAN: You were six.

JEAN: He was a good father. Tom worshipped him.

ADELE: Yes, he filled the breach, poor dead Archie.

> *(JEAN and ADELE laugh.)*

YOUNG JEAN: I don't know how you can laugh about it!

JEAN: How else can you deal with death?

YOUNG JEAN: No...I mean, being married to Archie.

JEAN: Oh, that. It wasn't so bad.

YOUNG JEAN: You might have found somebody...better.

JEAN: In my dreams.

ADELE: Mary's going to be devastated tonight, when you get
                  up there all denuded.

JEAN: *(Sighs.)* She won't get past the mothballs.

> *(JEAN holds robes to ADELE's face; ADELE
> pushes her away, laughing.)*

ADELE: So where's the benediction?

JEAN: In my head.

ADELE: Better write it out. You'll forget.

> *(JEAN and YOUNG JEAN are moving off a bit.)*

JEAN:	I'm going off the cuff. I've been collecting phrases all summer. Been at it since May. Never had your unholy alliance with words though; when I speak they come out bald. You were famous for yours.
ADELE:	My what.
JEAN:	Words.
ADELE:	Where was I famous.
JEAN:	Everywhere. Because of your book. I'll bring it out for you when I leave.
ADELE:	Don't bother.
JEAN:	Anyway, it's been fifteen summers since I was ordained. It's not going to be sixteen.
ADELE:	You have to make this one count. So write it out!
YOUNG JEAN:	Hold on here! We were fighting the church! Priests, bishops...religion!
JEAN:	It wasn't religion we were against.
YOUNG JEAN:	And now you've bought into the whole lie!
JEAN:	It was just the way religion was behaving itself. In Spain. And environs. But things can change, and for the better. You're so old-fashioned in your prejudices. It's your youth. Optimism scares you. *(To ADELE.)* I have to stand up there and make the words waltz like you made them, and they have to be for Tom and for our grandson...
ADELE:	Jeffy.
JEAN:	And the granddaughters. Uh.
ADELE:	Whatsit and Whosit.
JEAN:	I don't want their last memory of me to be me standing there, looking like Pocahantas' worst nightmare.

(*JEAN and YOUNG JEAN move off a bit. Focus is on YOUNG ADELE and PAUL, setting up mah-jongg tiles. They are sitting reasonably close to ADELE.*)

YOUNG ADELE: Your family...you have one?

PAUL: Yes.

YOUNG ADELE: And they're exotic?

PAUL: Uh...not the word I'd use.

YOUNG ADELE: Exiled nobility.

PAUL: In Saskatchewan?

YOUNG ADELE: European nobles on the lam on the trackless prairie.

PAUL: Try a socialist preacher with a bitter wife. Try four scared kids. Try about twenty pulpits in twenty stinking villages. You know what my chief memory is? Looking out the back window of our Dodge, watching the gravel spit up as another town fades off. Dad purged from yet another pulpit because he never learned to tell them what they wanted to hear. But that's him, that's a world away. You don't want to know about it.

YOUNG ADELE: I do.

PAUL: I don't want to tell it.

YOUNG ADELE: Why.

PAUL: You'll put it into blank verse. Come on. Tell me about McGill.

YOUNG ADELE: Nothing to tell. I took the required subjects. Lived in residence. We played bridge. Every night. I'm afraid that's my chief memory. Bridge. Did you? Play?

PAUL: No.

YOUNG ADELE: Did Jean. In her dorm?

PAUL: I doubt it.

YOUNG ADELE: Does she have a nice room?

PAUL: I've never seen it.

YOUNG ADELE: We were very good at smuggling men into ours.

PAUL: Perhaps the University of Toronto is stricter about those things.

YOUNG ADELE: She's a good worker. I'm not surprised she's gone off to the factory. And I'm sorry about my little temper the other day. But I miss her.

PAUL: Yes.

YOUNG ADELE: And you...do you miss her?

PAUL: Of course.

YOUNG ADELE: Jean's very close-mouthed about things.

PAUL: Then ask me.

YOUNG ADELE: Ask what.

PAUL: What you so desperately want to ask.

YOUNG ADELE: Are you?

PAUL: No.

YOUNG ADELE: Not at all?

PAUL: No.

YOUNG ADELE: Do you want to be?

PAUL: Does she?

YOUNG ADELE: Yes.

PAUL: Is that what she said?

YOUNG ADELE: That's for me to know. Do you find her pretty?

PAUL: Jean and I raise money to send volunteers to Spain. We're good at it. We work hard. I'm chairman of the campus group, Jean's treasurer. We go to class, separately, then we go out and raise money. Together. We're not involved.

YOUNG ADELE: She wants to be.

(PAUL grabs YOUNG ADELE's arm.)

PAUL: What do you want from me?

(YOUNG ADELE shakes him off.)

YOUNG ADELE: Nothing.

PAUL: Don't lie.

(PAUL grabs YOUNG ADELE's arm again.)

You've been after something ever since Jean left for the city.

YOUNG ADELE: Don't flatter yourself.

PAUL: I know what it is.

YOUNG ADELE: I don't like my tiles.

(YOUNG ADELE knocks down the wall of tiles.)

You don't know a damn thing.

(PAUL grabs her harder this time, and holds her wrist up.)

PAUL: I know all about you rich girls.

YOUNG ADELE: *(Imitating.)* Ah...now it's a class struggle.

PAUL: With one notable exception, I've discovered rich girls can't tell the truth.

YOUNG ADELE: Why bother? The proletariat never listens.

PAUL: I know that rich girls get what they want.

YOUNG ADELE: Why not? We deserve it.

PAUL: Until you get what you deserve. But I look at your cousin and I have hope. When I look at you...

YOUNG ADELE: You see what?

(PAUL has moved his hand from clenching YOUNG ADELE's wrist, and has moved it to her hand.)

You think it's that easy.

(PAUL lets her hand go.)

The steamer will be dropping Jean off any minute. Swim back there to her. Tell her I'm looking forward to hearing about the first fortnight at the factory. Tell her I'm dying to hear about the industrial revolution.

(YOUNG ADELE pushes the rest of the mah-jongg tiles over. She pulls PAUL to her and kisses him hard. PAUL and YOUNG ADELE exit, in opposite directions. ADELE has stayed alert and is admiring the mah-jongg tiles. JEAN returns, carrying ADELE's book and wearing her now-correct robes.)

ADELE: What's that.

JEAN: Your book.

ADELE: Why're you tormenting me with that now! It's a slim

excuse for a life. Allegorical fluff. *(Pause.)* Does anyone still read it?

JEAN: Of course.

ADELE: Liar. I know what they say. The naturalists hate it because the animals talk. The kids hate it because it's not TV and no one gets killed. The women's libbers hate it because the men hunt and the women cook.

JEAN: Stop it!

ADELE: It's the truth!

JEAN: *(Reads.)* "Seamless rock. Buckling pine. There are a million rustlings in the dark, a hundred thousand trips of the heart." You were smart to write it for children. They understand it on a level we never could.

ADELE: Oh, cut the pretty-pretty, Jean.

JEAN: You won awards!

ADELE: I wrote a damn kids' book that a bunch of stupid wankers decided was important.

JEAN: You touched a million readers. Young and old.

ADELE: With vacant gibberish. Entire forests died so my book could gather dust on library shelves. For God's sake, Jean, I'm dying! Don't bury me with cheerleading!

JEAN: "We lived in harmony once and one day peace would return to the island but not today."

             (Suddenly ADELE sits bolt upright, her arms pressed about her.)

ADELE: Jean. Jean!

JEAN: What is it?

ADELE: I need you! You have to help me! You have to help me out of this.

(JEAN is pushing ADELE back down.)

JEAN: It's OK, it's all right.

ADELE: What can I do!

JEAN: Stop thrashing. Calm down. Calm down. There.

(ADELE begins to quieten.)

ADELE: I've made such a mess.

JEAN: It's fixed. I'm fixing it. You lie there, I'll fix it all. Now I'm going to get you another drink. I'll be right back.

(JEAN goes inside. ADELE doesn't exactly watch the following, but is aware. YOUNG ADELE appears down centre, holding a lamp. She is wearing a kimono. PAUL comes out of the water. He walks towards here. PAUL and YOUNG ADELE meet, kiss, begin making love, for the first time.

The lamp dims, light coming back up on ADELE. JEAN emerges, with drink. JEAN sits beside ADELE and props her up gently.)

It's OK. There. Drink this. Take a sip.

(ADELE reaches for the glass, taking it with both hands. She is helped by JEAN.)

Drink. Drink. Drink.

(Light fades to black. End of ACT ONE.)

ACT TWO

(YOUNG ADELE and PAUL are sitting on ADELE's chaise. It is very clear they are lovers. ADELE is lying behind them, not yet visible.)

YOUNG ADELE: Hard to imagine there was nothing here once but ice. Until just 12,000 years ago.

PAUL: Give or take an era.

YOUNG ADELE: All of a sudden the glacier went north.

PAUL: Looking for whatever hunks of ice seek.

YOUNG ADELE: Gin? And now people come here to study these rocks. Specialists. Trying to figure out why the glaciers ever wanted to leave.

(Kissing gets a bit heavier.)

PAUL: I don't want to leave, ever.

(Kissing gets heavier.)

YOUNG ADELE: Then don't.

(ADELE becomes visible behind them.)

ADELE: I've died and gone to heaven.

(PAUL and YOUNG ADELE turn to her and are laughing.)

YOUNG ADELE: You wish.

PAUL: Anyway, I thought you hated me.

ADELE: From a distance. Hey…watch my drink. Jean'll have a fit if it's knocked over. She'll think I'm procrastinating.

                (PAUL and YOUNG ADELE have started eyeing each other again.)

                As you were.

PAUL: I won't leave here.

YOUNG ADELE: Maybe I will.

PAUL: When.

YOUNG ADELE: The minute you start making rules. I'll leave.

ADELE: Liar.

YOUNG ADELE: Don't interrupt.

ADELE: You'll stay away for decades.

YOUNG ADELE: Please?

ADELE: When Jean's bringing up Tom and it drives you mental watching her; you'll come up in the spring and the fall but the summer will be too painful.

YOUNG ADELE: *(To ADELE.)* Can I just have this moment with him?

PAUL: So you're telling me I'm not the first guy in your life.

ADELE: That's a laugh.

YOUNG ADELE: You already knew that.

PAUL: Are you telling me I won't be the last?

YOUNG ADELE: I could never be that honest with you.

ADELE: You won't be the last. Not by a long shot. And you're nowhere near the best, either.

PAUL: You've gotten awfully crabby in your old age.

ADELE: OK, you're in the top ten.

PAUL: *(Kissing ADELE.)* Top ten? Come on...

ADELE: Top four. We're not falling for this. Top two.

PAUL: *(To YOUNG ADELE.)* These past weeks...I've seen a whole new side to you. Jean always described you as a party girl, but that's not you.

ADELE: *(To YOUNG ADELE.)* It's a line.

YOUNG ADELE: What am I?

PAUL: You're an artist. There's a sadness in you, a love for place, something that runs as deep as the back channel, something that makes you restless.

ADELE: Soon he's going to say you dazzle him.

YOUNG ADELE: It's true I've got lots of friends at McGill...true that I went to a million parties and dances. But it never brought me comfort, never. I'd go up to the mountain, and I'll look down at the river.

ADELE: And squint through blurred eyes...

PAUL: Tears.

ADELE: I could almost imagine, just about imagine I was here.

YOUNG ADELE: Just about but not quite. *(To ADELE.)* That much is true, isn't it?

ADELE: It's true, all right. All those years I spent in exile because I couldn't bear to look across that bit of water and see my Tom. Growing up. Over there. Not here. Couldn't stand the guilt. Or the wanting to tell him, wanting so badly to just let it drop. Casually. In a conversation. "You're mine, actually." But I'd see him growing up so happy, so happy over there. I couldn't interfere with that.

YOUNG ADELE: This year...even my poetry was lonely. I'd put a word here, a word there. Nothing connected. I was living my year in blank verse, a bit of pleasure here, a

moment of happiness there. How many words do you
need?

ADELE: Not many. *(Recovering a bit, indicates environs.)* It's
gotten run-down, eh?

PAUL: I hadn't noticed.

ADELE: I like it better this way. Jean would send one of the
locals over to do maintenance. Sometimes I'd rent it
out. By the time I started coming back, it was tilting
and rotting and...

PAUL: It reminds me of all the manses I lived in out
west...except there's a difference between choosing
shabby and having it forced on you.

YOUNG ADELE: I don't understand.

PAUL: Jean would.

YOUNG ADELE: I doubt it.

                *(ADELE makes a noise, indicating some degree
                of disagreement, as well.)*

                It's ironic. She's so practical and now she's in the
                factory, creating beauty. Beauty en masse...hundreds
                of boats lined up, waiting for finish, impatient to be
                launched into uncharted waters. And above it all, the
                air...dust, sawdust making the air tangible. The sun
                cutting through it like a gold shaft, giving it that glow
                like the best dream of an Old Master.

PAUL: When I dreamed, when I was able to dream, I dreamt
                of you. Of here. I didn't know that before. I know it
                now.

                *(PAUL and YOUNG ADELE slip off a bit, and
                are in front of ADELE. They begin making love.
                JEAN enters and picks her way carefully around
                them. JEAN props up ADELE with some
                difficulty, as ADELE now seems a bit weaker,*

perhaps sleepier. PAUL and YOUNG ADELE will move off.)

JEAN: Not time to sleep yet. I want you to have some food, and watch the flotilla go over to St. Pete's.

ADELE: With all our American friends.

(YOUNG JEAN emerges from the dock area. She is dressed in city clothes, and she runs towards the cottage area.)

YOUNG JEAN: Addie! Paul! Addie!

ADELE: You know, we heard you coming.

YOUNG JEAN: Addie!

(YOUNG JEAN goes off, into cottage area, keeps calling.)

JEAN: Who's we?

YOUNG ADELE: Paul and I. *(Indicating ADELE.)* She tells me he's going to be a professor of Political Thought.

JEAN: He was.

ADELE: And he never did go to Spain.

JEAN: There wouldn't have been much use, really. Not by '38. He'd've been cannon fodder. No one was surviving long by then.

ADELE: He could've gone in '37. Or '36. He didn't have to stay in school. He didn't have to come here.

JEAN: He was meant to come here. He was meant to stand on these rocks like a sign at a roadfork, pointing me one way, you the other. But that's all he was. A fork in the road.

ADELE: Ah Jean…I've lived a foolish, selfish life.

JEAN: So? I wrecked a boat company.

ADELE: I wrote a stupid book with talking animals.

JEAN: I went into politics and got the stuffing kicked out of me.

ADELE: My book did sell millions.

JEAN: Then I went into the ministry and closed churches.

ADELE: Plus you spent forty years sharing a bed with Archie Copeland! You should be drinking this by the bucket! *(Pause.)* But you raised Tom. And you have grandchildren. Jeffy, those girls, whatever their damn names are, Hoojee and Whatsee. And you've spent the summer taking care of me when someone should've been looking after you.

                    (JEAN hands her a drink.)

                    Already?

                    (YOUNG JEAN has found YOUNG ADELE and PAUL by the water. They've quickly produced a deck of cards. PAUL stands when YOUNG JEAN appears.)

YOUNG JEAN: You're way out here!

PAUL: How's our weary worker?

YOUNG JEAN: Did you get my postcard? Oh God, I've got so much to tell you. Two weeks. *(Pulls out a cigarette; offers.)* Feels like a lifetime! How are you both? Enough small talk; let me tell you about Kawartha Canoe.

PAUL: You built your first runabout.

YOUNG JEAN: They won't let me near a machine. I report to Will Copeland. Archie's Dad.

YOUNG ADELE: Who makes Archie look frantic.

(JEAN will soon edge closer to hear. She will react, under some of YOUNG JEAN. Mostly a mixture of genuine pride and a bit of ruefulness at her past naivete.)

YOUNG JEAN: Except at the plant. He's the general manager. He's a petty despot. You wouldn't believe how he treats people!

PAUL: Isn't there a union?

YOUNG JEAN: Yes, but it's Sweetheart. The stewards are either scared out of their minds by Copeland or, I suspect, bought off.

PAUL: It must drive you nuts.

YOUNG JEAN: It'll be changed.

PAUL: What's he got you doing?

YOUNG JEAN: Mostly boring stuff. Filing, petty cash. Medical reports. But they let me read everything and I can walk through the plant and talk to anyone I like. The foremen aren't exactly going to complain and, anyway, I spend a lot of time talking to them. This is in my blood!

YOUNG ADELE: Are you OK?

YOUNG JEAN: One day it's going to be mine and...

YOUNG ADELE: She's running a fever.

YOUNG JEAN: Where else is it going! My father's 64, yours is 58. I'm an only child, you're an only child. You don't care about the place. I do. So it's mine.

(JEAN is watching, proudly.)

(To PAUL.) You know how I've been talking about connecting my head and my heart, how working for Spain filled that...well, this is another way. The difference is, at Kawartha I'm not plodding about

begging nickels...here I can make real changes. But...I'm getting ahead of myself. You have to see the plant. The boats are beautiful. Hiatus is top of the line. Mostly we build smaller boats—outboards, runabouts, cedar strip canoes. It was Dad's decision...leave the luxury market to others and we go after general sales. And, now the Depression's ending, everyone's building cottages, sales are booming...

PAUL: *(Bemused.)* Beauty to the masses?

YOUNG JEAN: Except we create that beauty in squalor!

YOUNG ADELE: We do not!

YOUNG JEAN: The plant is out of the dark ages!

YOUNG ADELE: How can you say that!

YOUNG JEAN: It's everything we're against!

YOUNG ADELE: It's the most modern...

YOUNG JEAN: The machinery is huge and noisy. The saws take your ears off and we don't supply the men with plugs.

JEAN: There are accidents.

YOUNG ADELE: There's a company doctor!

JEAN: Who couldn't heal a dog.

YOUNG JEAN: In the paint shop the varnish fumes strip your lungs. Imagine breathing that for forty years.

JEAN: Even today there's men in Ashburnham General with lung problems that began there, forty years ago.

YOUNG JEAN: They get a half hour for lunch and they eat in a stuffy room just off the plant floor, in all that bad air. Even though there's a perfectly good park down the street.

YOUNG ADELE: Which we donated to the city!

YOUNG JEAN: The men who made us the money we donated can't use it!

YOUNG ADELE: Our fathers made that money! It was their sweat and their brains.

JEAN: Whose sweat?

PAUL: The workers did nothing?

YOUNG ADELE: They wouldn't have been there but for our fathers! They'd be...out riding the rails for all I know. Volunteering for Spain. *(To YOUNG JEAN.)* You're being an ass. You should be more loyal. *(Back to PAUL.)* It's not nearly that bad. They make beautiful boats, which give thousands of people transport and pleasure. It also makes money which buys islands, builds cottages, pays tuition, allows her to run about Toronto gathering her revolutionary nickels.

PAUL: Have you talked with any of the workers?

YOUNG JEAN: That's the best part! They...some...a few...talk to me. They don't all treat me like I'm the boss's daughter. They resent the fact no one listens to them. They have ideas. Ideas on how to build boats even better and more safely, really good ideas about design that no one listens to.

YOUNG ADELE: Now it's Daddy's fault!

YOUNG JEAN: It's the way the place is set up! The designers who work for your father don't dare go to him with their ideas. They think we should start a line of aluminum boats!

YOUNG ADELE: Aluminum!

YOUNG JEAN: Why not!

YOUNG ADELE: Daddy will just love designing in aluminum.

ADELE: You were so practical.

(JEAN upon hearing ADELE, remembers her duties.)

YOUNG JEAN: He may have no choice one day. You can press out an aluminum boat in five minutes.

ADELE: You wanted to switch to tin but the workers didn't.

JEAN: Drink.

ADELE: You were right, of course.

YOUNG JEAN: There's something else.

ADELE: They were so afraid of change. Imagine being so afraid of anything but the status quo, you end up doing yourself in.

JEAN: Read the papers. Whole nations are doing it.

ADELE: They were dinosaurs.

JEAN: Drink.

YOUNG JEAN: I'm not going back to school!

(Silence. All four look at YOUNG JEAN.)

ADELE: Oh oh.

JEAN: I could've lead into it better.

YOUNG JEAN: I'm going to stay on at Kawartha Canoe! I'm going to learn everything a person can learn about the business: design, management, marketing. I'm going to make myself an expert.

JEAN: Right on!

(They all swivel and stare at JEAN.)

PAUL: But Jean

YOUNG JEAN: Let me finish

JEAN: Slap your cards down!

YOUNG JEAN: In a decade or so, when it's all mine, I'm going to convert it.

YOUNG ADELE: To tin can boats? Whoopee!

YOUNG JEAN: To a worker's co-operative.

(Pause.)

ADELE: Oh boy.

JEAN: The shit's going to hit the fan now.

YOUNG JEAN: Workers will be owners and owners will be workers.

JEAN: *(Over last.)* "And owners will be workers." I can't believe I said that.

YOUNG ADELE: Are you out of your mind?

ADELE: Yes, that's me.

YOUNG ADELE: That is the dumbest idea I've ever heard.

PAUL: Are you serious?

YOUNG JEAN: Dead serious.

ADELE: In your next career as I recall...

JEAN: Don't bother

ADELE: It was "Voters will be legislators."

JEAN: "Trust the public."

YOUNG JEAN: It's not as if it's a new idea. There are co-ops springing up all over.

YOUNG ADELE: Where? Spain? Are they featuring canoe co-ops in Barcelona these days? Two weeks at a factory you've ignored for twenty-one years and now you're going to change the world. I hope you haven't mentioned this to your father.

JEAN: Thank God he died before I took it over...

YOUNG JEAN: I still have to tell him I'm quitting school.

ADELE: That alone nearly killed him.

YOUNG ADELE: You've gone 'round the bend.

PAUL:	It's an interesting plan.
YOUNG JEAN:	"Interesting"?
JEAN:	*(With her.)* "Interesting"!
PAUL:	It's a big step.
YOUNG ADELE:	Backwards.
YOUNG JEAN:	I knew she wouldn't understand.
ADELE:	You could be such a prig.
JEAN:	Drink.
PAUL:	You've unloaded a lot on us.
YOUNG JEAN:	She wouldn't understand if I gave her all summer.
YOUNG ADELE:	You're acting like a twelve year-old.
YOUNG JEAN:	I'd hoped you'd be a little excited for me, or at least keep an open mind *(To PAUL.)* But you heard. If I'd marched back from the factory with the latest shade of working girl lipstick, that might've got her onside. Mewled a little blank verse I overheard in that lunch hellhole, she'd have thought me very *au courant* and the factory just the goddamn bees knees. But no. I have a plan. Plans require thought. Then they require commitment.

(YOUNG ADELE is stalking off.)

And there she goes.

YOUNG ADELE:	I've had enough insults.

(YOUNG ADELE exits, but pauses briefly before leaving. Looks at PAUL. PAUL avoids her look. YOUNG ADELE exits.)

JEAN/ADELE:	Five four three two one.

(But YOUNG ADELE only comes and watches PAUL and YOUNG JEAN.)

YOUNG JEAN: No?

PAUL: She's upset.

YOUNG JEAN: I'm upset!

PAUL: But maybe you should

YOUNG JEAN: I'm the one with the idea!

JEAN: She won't even consider it.

PAUL: You're too harsh with her.

YOUNG JEAN: What!

PAUL: She only needs educating! She's worried about you. I worry about you.

JEAN: Right.

YOUNG JEAN: You do.

PAUL: Of course!

YOUNG JEAN: But you know I can do this. Don't you? You've seen what I can do when I put my mind to it.

PAUL: Yes, but...

YOUNG JEAN: Then why aren't you supporting me!

PAUL: I am!

YOUNG JEAN: It doesn't sound like it from here.

JEAN: Or here.

PAUL: I worry that when you get involved with a company like your family's, you'll lose your perspective. We all start with high goals, but business co-opts people.

JEAN: Nuts! Nuts!

(JEAN is exiting in disgust. YOUNG ADELE continues to watch.)

PAUL: Perhaps the only way we can keep our integrity is by working for change from the outside.

YOUNG JEAN: Oh that really makes sense. And when change finally happens—scary thought—what do you do, sit back, retire?

PAUL: I'm just saying...

YOUNG JEAN: I know exactly what you're saying! You think I'll walk through the portals of Kawartha Canoe and transform into a raging capitalist. But I'm different. I'm...different. Perhaps that happens to others, but it won't happen to me. If you don't think my principles are strong enough, if you can't believe they won't stand up, maybe it's because.... No. Listen to me. Paul, I can walk in there and *(Snaps fingers.)* I can start implementing. I don't have to spend years working my way up and...I have the power.

PAUL: Think about that, too. With one flick of your hankie you can become Lady Bountiful.

YOUNG JEAN: It's irrelevant what I have!

PAUL: Are you sure?

YOUNG JEAN: It only matters how I use it.

PAUL: You're rich. I'm not. It's easy for you.

YOUNG JEAN: Easy? Easy! What's ever been easy? Who are you to say what's easy! Who slaved all year fundraising? Who kept the books, who set up the halls for you to speak in? I just about lost my year, for you, for the cause, for what we were doing. Easy? This isn't easy. Easy would be to do that. *(Points to where YOUNG ADELE went.)* Easy is being an artist. Easy is sitting on the dock pondering life in goddamn blank verse. *(Pause.)* Don't you see, don't you understand how much I need your support now that I have a plan. Turnabout is fair play, Paul. I need your support. I need you to say, "Do it ."

PAUL:	Yes, OK, yes. Do it. You must do it.
YOUNG JEAN:	It's not that crazy.
PAUL:	It's a good plan.
YOUNG JEAN:	And yes, it did only occur to me these past two weeks, but it's not as if I haven't been laying the groundwork all my life.
PAUL:	It's a good plan. Come here.
YOUNG JEAN:	And I can do it. I will do it.
PAUL:	Come here.

(PAUL puts his arms out, pulls YOUNG JEAN to him. He smiles. ADELE is now watching, along with YOUNG ADELE.)

It's an amazing plan.

(PAUL holds YOUNG JEAN again.)

YOUNG JEAN:	You support me, don't you?
PAUL:	I do.
YOUNG JEAN:	It didn't sound like it, for a minute.
PAUL:	I wanted to see how serious you were. We should go back.
YOUNG JEAN:	*(Of cards and things.)* I should take these up.
PAUL:	Better not to go near Addie right now. Bring them with us. I'll drop them over tomorrow, after your steamer goes.

(YOUNG JEAN exits. PAUL goes to ADELE. JEAN comes back and watches with YOUNG ADELE. After a while she will emerge. She mixes another drink. PAUL hovers near ADELE. When

he does, she is calm and wakeful. When he leaves she becomes more agitated.)

ADELE: It's not me, it's my island.

PAUL: *(Kissing her.)* It casts a spell on prairie boys. Makes them act out of character.

ADELE: Hah. The spell won't last. The minute you're back in Toronto you'll forget the breeze hissing, you'll forget Hiatus groaning against the dock.

PAUL: I'll remember me against you.

ADELE: I'll never forget this.

PAUL: "Never forgetting" implies something has ended.

ADELE: Jean says you're only a fork in the road.

PAUL: What do you think?

ADELE: Will you ever go to Spain?

PAUL: I'm too late.

ADELE: Will you really become a bitter old professor?

PAUL: With hair in my ears?

ADELE: And you died on a croquet battlefield?

PAUL: According to Jean. *(Caressing ADELE.)* but don't you believe a word of it. I'm off to organise unions in Guatemala.

ADELE: *(Sadly.)* Damn you.

PAUL: I'll be running a little bar for radicals on Capri.

ADELE: Damn you.

PAUL: I'm surprised you've never visited. It's very lovely.

ADELE: You know, I never had another man up here, after you. Seems like a waste of a good island now.

(JEAN has come over. PAUL moves off a bit.)

JEAN: Drink this. It's nearly time. *(To PAUL.)* Get lost.

ADELE: You did a terrible thing.

JEAN: You can eat out here and then you won't miss the boat parade, and the sunset.

ADELE: Why didn't you at least tell me where he was?

(JEAN hands ADELE a drink.)

JEAN: Uh—you'd have gone to see him.

ADELE: That was my decision to make! You never let me decide anything! You never let anyone decide anything!

JEAN: I've learned, from bitter experience, that it's better when I make the decisions.

ADELE: Don't you know what that does to people!

JEAN: There was a boat company, need I remind you, that went belly-up because the workers wouldn't allow it to modernise. There was a young woman who God knows what would've happened to her if I hadn't taken over.

ADELE: So to save some pain then, I listened to you, did what you said, and paid for it for the last fifty years, paid for it because I had to sit here and watch you raise Tom...

JEAN: And raise him well! Better than you would have, and you know that. *(Pause.)* And now there's two old women, one dying, the other hot on her heels and if I wasn't deciding for us again, where would we be?

ADELE: Well, I've changed my mind.

JEAN: It's too late.

ADELE: I'm not ready.

JEAN: We can't turn back now. It's all in motion. This is our
                   last chance. Tom wants to drive us into town
                   tomorrow.

ADELE: *(Throws drink down.)* We can stop.

JEAN: No!

ADELE: I'm not the one dying! You're the one with cancer! I
                   could sit here for years.

JEAN: Except it won't be here. Surely you don't believe
                   they'll let you stay here after I'm gone! Who's going
                   to take care of you? Tom? He wanted me to slap you
                   in a Home after your first stroke. The grandchildren?
                   They think you're an eccentric old fool!! You can't
                   go back to Montreal; there's no one to line up the
                   homecare or bang down your door and rescue you
                   after your next stroke. Addie, Addie, if I thought for
                   one second we could make it to another summer, if we
                   could come back here one more time... There's no
                   alternative. We've talked and talked about this. This
                   is our last day of control. There is no other way!

                   *(JEAN goes in. ADELE is exhausted, and lies
                   back. PAUL is hovering within ADELE's range
                   of vision. YOUNG ADELE emerges, carrying an
                   oil lamp. ADELE watches for a while, and then
                   drifts off.)*

YOUNG ADELE: Jean and I used to send each other signals across the
                   channel. *(Puts a board in front of the lamp.)* Three
                   quick flashes means, "Parents in bed, coast clear."
                   She'd hop in Hiatus and come over. You can swim.

PAUL: It's too risky.

YOUNG ADELE: She'll never know. She's exhausted from the
                   industrial revolution. She'll be out like a light. But
                   swim over. I want that. For you to come out of water.

                   *(YOUNG ADELE and PAUL move off in
                   opposite directions. PAUL passes ADELE,*

touching her. ADELE speaks to his departed presence.)

ADELE: She did a good job raising Tom. And that dolt Archie made a surprisingly good father. Really took an interest in the boy. Tom's martinis are the envy of the lake. And the grandchildren.... Tom's girls are the two best looking things on the lake, and that boy...he's going to break some hearts. *(Pause.)* Nevertheless.

(It is late evening. YOUNG ADELE comes to the front rock lights the lamp, covers it three times. JEAN is bringing food to ADELE.)

YOUNG ADELE: *(Murmuring.)* Oh you stars, you scattering stars...

(JEAN breaks off a chunk of bread, peels the crust, hands it to ADELE.)

JEAN: Take this and eat.

(ADELE eats bread. JEAN hands her a glass.)

Take this and drink.

(PAUL emerges from the lake. He goes to YOUNG ADELE and lies down beside her. They kiss, and begin making love.)

ADELE: Can one person really change your life that much?

JEAN: It's the choices you make afterwards.

ADELE: Or the choices people make for you.

JEAN: Yes. I'm sorry. There's no alternative.

(YOUNG JEAN appears. ADELE and JEAN are riveted by her appearance. Their ritual is suspended.)

JEAN: Oh go home. Go home.

ADELE: You can try all you want.

JEAN: Go home.

ADELE: Can't change things now. Can't go back now.

JEAN: Jeannie...

(YOUNG JEAN goes over to YOUNG ADELE and PAUL.)

PAUL: Jesus!

YOUNG ADELE: Jean!

PAUL: What are you doing here!

YOUNG JEAN: Three flashes means you want me...so I came.

YOUNG ADELE: Go home.

YOUNG JEAN: Odd you didn't hear me. But you were preoccupied.

YOUNG ADELE: GO HOME!

YOUNG JEAN: I'm not surprised. I'm not. Really. I can't sleep; I'm walking along the shoreline; I see three flashes. I go to the dock. His clothes are piled there. That's called a clue. Like all the other clues I've been too stupid to see you scattering these past weeks. *(To YOUNG ADELE.)* Go inside.

YOUNG ADELE: No.

YOUNG JEAN: I'll deal with you later.

YOUNG ADELE: I'm not going.

(YOUNG JEAN makes a physical threat.)

PAUL: You better go.

YOUNG ADELE: We can talk about this.

YOUNG JEAN: I don't think so.

PAUL: It's OK, go. I'll see you tomorrow.

YOUNG JEAN: *(To YOUNG ADELE.)* It's really none of your concern.

(YOUNG ADELE runs off, and joins JEAN and ADELE. YOUNG JEAN stares at PAUL.)

YOUNG JEAN: I'm not quite sure what to do.

PAUL: Listen to me.

YOUNG JEAN: That's the one thing I won't do.

PAUL: We should've told you.

YOUNG JEAN: I don't care about this. This is not important to me. I don't care if you're...if you're doing this with her the minute I go into town.

(JEAN is coming over.)

But every time I've turned my back...God I've tried not to notice, to think about this...every time I turn around, even when I turn real slow...even when I try and warn you I'm going to turn around and see...you're not there. You're just not there. You don't care about Spain. You don't care about fighting facism. You don't care about social justice or me creating a workers co-op...

JEAN: You just want to screw my cousin.

PAUL: It's not screwing.

JEAN: What is it then?

PAUL: It's not screwing when I love her.

YOUNG JEAN: LIAR!

JEAN: You never loved her!

YOUNG JEAN: How many others are there! Tell her that!

PAUL: She's different.

JEAN: She's the same as all the rest!

YOUNG JEAN: I didn't want to see them either.

> *(YOUNG ADELE and ADELE are watching.
> YOUNG ADELE has perhaps handed ADELE
> her blanket, and is comforting her.)*

JEAN: Get off this island!

YOUNG JEAN: Go!

> *(PAUL exits in direction of the lake. YOUNG
> JEAN falls into JEAN's arms, and sobs.)*

JEAN: It's OK.

YOUNG JEAN: I hate him.

JEAN: Say what you really mean.

YOUNG JEAN: I hate him.

JEAN: Say what you mean!

YOUNG JEAN: *(Pulling herself together.)* Never. Never. *(Pause.)*
                 Are you coming?

> *(YOUNG JEAN goes to boat area. JEAN follows.
> Light more up on ADELE and YOUNG ADELE.
> Underneath, the rumble of Hiatus starting up.)*

ADELE:	Jean has something up her sleeve.
YOUNG ADELE:	You'd think she'd have learned by now.
ADELE:	She was born to play God. Born so. But this is beyond her powers even.

(YOUNG JEAN is driving Hiatus, standing up. Spray in her face. JEAN stands beside her. They speak over and under each other, and sometimes in unison.)

YOUNG JEAN:	I know where you're swimming...
JEAN:	He's going down the back channel...
YOUNG JEAN:	You're swimming for your clothes...
JEAN:	He'll cross at the point...
YOUNG JEAN:	Clothes you take off for her...
JEAN:	You don't need to sweep that way—go straight...
YOUNG JEAN:	I know every rock and log in this channel...
JEAN:	Get him...
YOUNG JEAN:	I know them all...
JEAN:	Over there!
YOUNG JEAN:	Moon on rock, rock and pine...
JEAN:	Look! There!
YOUNG JEAN:	Your arms. Forking up.
JEAN:	Cutting down...
YOUNG JEAN:	Your head, black dot, arms glistening in moonlight, forking up...
JEAN:	Cutting down, head dipping, pulling in...
YOUNG JEAN:	Your good arms...

JEAN: Strong arms…

YOUNG JEAN: Your arms, your head, dipping in lifting out, your lips, your lips parting for air…

JEAN: *(Grabs wheel, pushes a bit, steering.)* Deadhead!

YOUNG JEAN: You can hear me. Bee-sting through water. Can you hear me?

JEAN: He sees us!

YOUNG JEAN: You turn and see me, see me, see…. You know, you know, what I want to do. I want to grind you into the water, into thick water, I want to bury you…

JEAN: Terror on his face…

YOUNG JEAN: You duck. You head to shore…

JEAN: Terror caught by moonlight

YOUNG JEAN: You dive! I turn! You head back! You turn! You duck! You surface…

PAUL: *(Rearing up.)* NO!

YOUNG JEAN: YES!

JEAN: NO!

PAUL: NO!

ADELE: *(Bolt upright.)* JEAN!

                    (YOUNG JEAN cuts Hiatus' engine, and leans forward, sobbing.)

ADELE: JEAN!

YOUNG JEAN: Oh God, what've I done!

                    (PAUL reaches over and hauls himself into the boat. YOUNG JEAN is trying to help him in. JEAN watches.)

I'm sorry. Oh God, I'm sorry, I'm sorry.

(YOUNG JEAN reaches to PAUL.)

I'm sorry, I'm sorry.

(PAUL hits YOUNG JEAN. She falls back into the boat. JEAN has a paddle. She winds up, hits PAUL with it. He falls into boat. She hits him, time and time again, in concert with YOUNG JEAN, until they are exhausted. She takes the wheel. Engine starts. She drives boat. Light up on ADELE.)

ADELE: Jean! Jean!

YOUNG ADELE: She'll be here.

ADELE: Jean!

YOUNG ADELE: She's just getting ready, she'll be right out.

ADELE: Help me Jeannie!

YOUNG ADELE: JEAN! JEANNIE!

(YOUNG ADELE restrains ADELE.)

ADELE: Help me!

YOUNG ADELE: Don't thrash about. Calm down. It's OK. Calm down.

ADELE: I don't want to do this!

YOUNG ADELE: It's too late!

(ADELE is quietening.)

Drink.

(YOUNG ADELE makes ADELE drink long and deeply. YOUNG JEAN has come out and stands beside YOUNG ADELE.)

YOUNG ADELE: You have to help me!

YOUNG JEAN: I am.

YOUNG ADELE: I can't go through with it!

YOUNG JEAN: Yes you can. I have a plan.

YOUNG ADELE: This happened to a girl at school. I was being careful.

YOUNG JEAN: So much for careful.

YOUNG ADELE: I was counting off the days...it always worked before.

YOUNG JEAN: You're going back to Montreal. People expect you to go back, and that's what you'll do. Nobody here will ever know you're not in school, why would they know? I'll come down with you and we'll find a flat.

YOUNG ADELE: If we knew where Paul was...

YOUNG JEAN: We don't.

YOUNG ADELE: Maybe he left a forwarding address with his landlady. You could check again. He has to know.

YOUNG JEAN: This is between you and me. He lost his rights when he assaulted me, when he sank Hiatus, when he sank it in the back channel, and when he took off. No, we do it this way, my way, or not at all. Understood?

YOUNG ADELE: Can't you stay with me...until the baby's born?

YOUNG JEAN: I'm going to marry Archie Copeland.

YOUNG ADELE: What!

YOUNG JEAN: I probably would've eventually.

YOUNG ADELE: But you hate him.

YOUNG JEAN: I know what hate is now and that's not what I feel for

Archie. He bores me, and suddenly that seems pretty benign. I'm going to stay on at the factory, Archie won't stand in the way of that. I can marry him at Christmas. A small wedding, you won't be able to come. We'll plead "exams". You're due in March. Archie and I can adopt.

YOUNG ADELE: Oh God, Jean, it's too...

YOUNG JEAN: Can you think of a better way?

YOUNG ADELE: How could you have thought of this!

YOUNG JEAN: We don't even need to tell Archie whose child it is.

YOUNG ADELE: He's not that thick!

(The four women look at each other and shrug.)

There'll be talk.

YOUNG JEAN: But no proof.

YOUNG ADELE: I want to tell Paul.

YOUNG JEAN: He's probably in Europe. He's probably on his way there. Right now. To Spain, I hope.

(JEAN has entered in her robes. Focus now back on JEAN and ADELE.)

JEAN: Finish eating so I can clean up.

ADELE: I don't think I can go this year.

JEAN: Of course you can't. You can watch the parade from here. *(Pause.)* We'll miss you though.

ADELE: Not half as much as I, you. I hate those robes all bare.

JEAN: Here's your book. *(Hands photograph.)* And Tom, your Tom. *(Another.)* Jeffy. It's a shame we never had a snap of Paul, to compare. Because there's a resemblance. One of me, when I was MP. Oh—I can hear the boat...that's Jeffy. Oh Jesus, Addie.

ADELE: Nothing much to say, is there.

JEAN: No.

ADELE: I love you.

JEAN: Ditto.

> *(ADELE is falling asleep. JEFFREY enters, a typically dressed teenager, including the inevitable baseball cap.)*

JEFFREY: Yo Gran!

> *(JEAN hushes him and points at ADELE.)*

She OK?

JEAN: She's exhausted. She's had a bad night, her worst, and she hasn't slept much. I'm leaving her out here; if she wakes up she can see the sunset and the parade.

JEFFREY: Won't she get cold?

JEAN: I've got her wrapped up.

> *(ADELE stirs.)*

I suppose we're going in that horrible boat.

JEFFREY: Full speed Gran.

ADELE: Paul?

JEAN: It's Jeffrey.

ADELE: Paul?

JEFFREY:	It's Jeff, Auntie. *(To JEAN.)* Who's Paul?
ADELE:	Why're you here?

(JEFFREY looks at JEAN, who shrugs.)

JEFFREY: I'm taking Gran to church.

(ADELE has drifted off again.)

Ready?

JEAN:	Ready.
JEFFREY:	*(Taking her arm.)* You stink of mothballs, Gran. Watch you don't trip.
JEAN:	Don't worry about me. You concentrate on driving that goddamn boat nice and slowly.

(ADELE stirs. Shifts a bit. JEAN sees her, stops. Turns to JEFFREY.)

Wait. Kiss her.

JEFFREY:	What?
JEAN:	Please. She'd like it.
JEFFREY:	She's asleep!
JEAN:	Please.

(JEFFREY looks doubtful, but he walks over to where ADELE is sleeping. JEAN has exited. JEFFREY leans down to kiss ADELE. He straightens, and removes his cap. He kisses ADELE on the cheek. ADELE's hand raises, as if to caress him. JEFFREY stands back up, then

*looks back at ADELE. He walks off. It becomes
dark. JEAN is standing on a flat rock. It slopes
gently to the water. She is wearing her robes and
her arms are raised in benediction.)*

Thick waters, seamless rock, buckling pine. Our
dazzling Kawartha sky, our unnumbered scatterings
of stars. Go in peace, my friends. Go in peace. Live
this year in happiness. Return in safety. God is close.
Carry him with you. Go now. Go.

*(JEAN stands in her robes, with the water around
her. Light comes up on ADELE, lying in her bed,
sheets, blankets white, her bed on the water's
edge. Moon is on the water. A long wind sigh.
Black.*

The End.)